T0011190

THE GREELY EXPEDITION'S FATAL QUEST FOR FARTHEST NORTH

by Golriz Golkar • illustrated by Ana Carolina Tega

CAPSTONE PRESS
a capstone imprint

Published by Capstone Press, an imprint of Capstone
1710 Roe Crest Drive, North Mankato, Minnesota 56003
capstonepub.com

Library of Congress Cataloging-in-Publication Data is available on the Library of
Congress website.

ISBN: 9781666390629 (hardcover)
ISBN: 9781666390575 (paperback)
ISBN: 9781666390582 (ebook PDF)

Summary: In 1881, the Greely expedition set sail for the Arctic on a mission to
collect polar climate data. They also had a second, secret goal: to achieve the
record of Farthest North. But when resupply ships failed to arrive two years
in a row, the team's dreams of glory turned into a nightmarish fight for survival.

Editorial Credits
Editor: Abby Huff; Designer: Dina Her; Production Specialist: Tori Abraham

All internet sites appearing in back matter were available and accurate when this
book was sent to press.

Printed and bound in the USA. PO5195

TABLE OF CONTENTS

On March 3, 1881, the U.S. Congress made a decision. For years, scientists had been asking for funding to study weather in the polar regions. Now, the United States agreed to help. The U.S. was joining 10 other countries. Together, the countries would build 14 research stations.

It will be good for America!

It's a waste of money!

The U.S. would build two stations. One would be in Alaska. The other would be near Lady Franklin Bay, about 600 miles from the North Pole. Some Congress members were against the expedition. Others saw an opportunity.

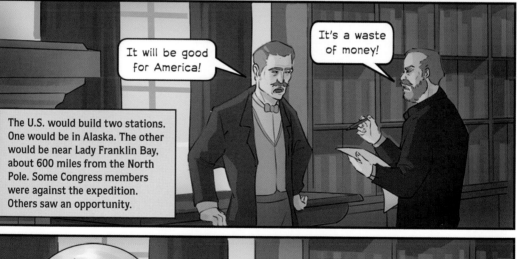

The Lady Franklin Bay team will have another, secret mission. To reach Farthest North!

Farthest North is the record for highest latitude reached by explorers. The British had held the record for centuries. The U.S. hoped to break it.

The U.S. Army Signal Corps would carry out the expedition. They often collected weather data across the country.

They chose Lieutenant Adolphus Greely to lead the Lady Franklin Bay team.

The journey will be dangerous!

My dear Henrietta, I shall help science *and* serve my country!

Greely was an experienced officer. He had fought for the Union in the Civil War. He later helped the army expand the U.S. telegraph network. This new invention was being used to track long-distance weather patterns.

With 25 officers, 2 Inuit guides, and a doctor, we have a fine crew!

On July 7, 1881, Greely and his men set sail. They left from St. John's, Newfoundland, Canada. For many of the crew, it was their first time at sea. For the army officers, it would be their first time ever in the Arctic.

After a smooth five-week journey, the crew arrived in Lady Franklin Bay. They stopped on the coast of Ellesmere Island. They unloaded 350 tons of food and supplies.

Almost no ice in the waters! Most unusual for this time of year.

Indeed, Lieutenant Lockwood! I feared ice might block our ship.

Unlike other polar expeditions, the crew would not keep their ship. It would soon leave. In a year, a ship would bring fresh supplies. In two years, a ship would bring the men home. Between those times, the men would have no connection to the outside world.

The crew built their headquarters, Fort Conger. They got ready to live and work in the harsh Arctic.

Greely was a respectful but strict leader.

Sergeant Brainard tells me there are no volunteers. Yet someone must wash our clothes!

I will, sir.

By mid-October, darkness set in. A long Arctic winter lay ahead. The men would not see daylight for nearly five months. Still, they worked tirelessly to collect weather data.

It's 25 degrees below zero!

What is the air pressure, sir?

29.7413 inches and holding steady.

They made 500 weather measurements every day.

What is the wind speed, sir?

17 miles per hour.

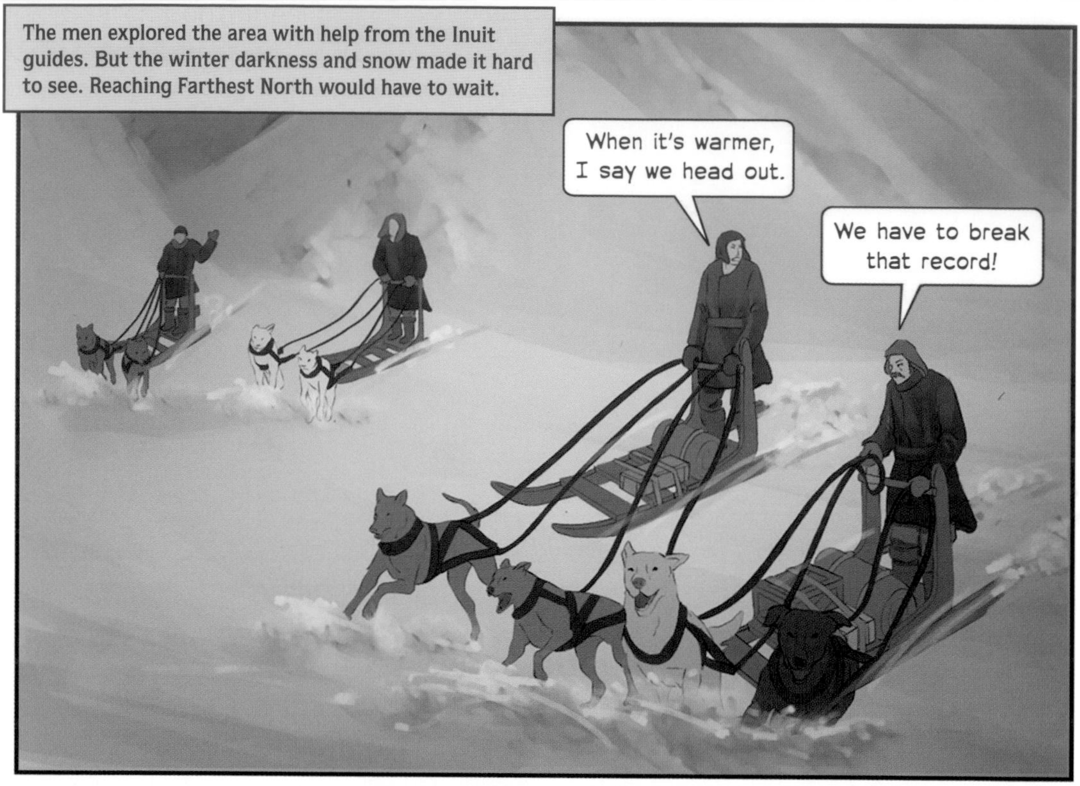
The men explored the area with help from the Inuit guides. But the winter darkness and snow made it hard to see. Reaching Farthest North would have to wait.
When it's warmer, I say we head out.
We have to break that record!

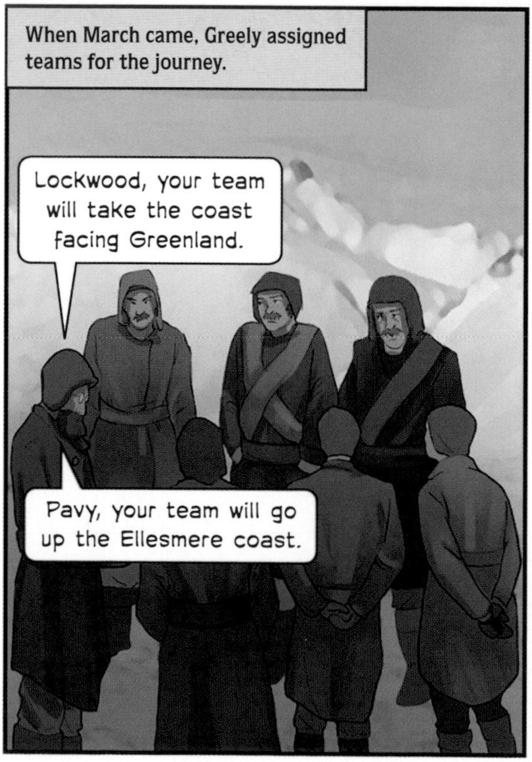
When March came, Greely assigned teams for the journey.
Lockwood, your team will take the coast facing Greenland.
Pavy, your team will go up the Ellesmere coast.

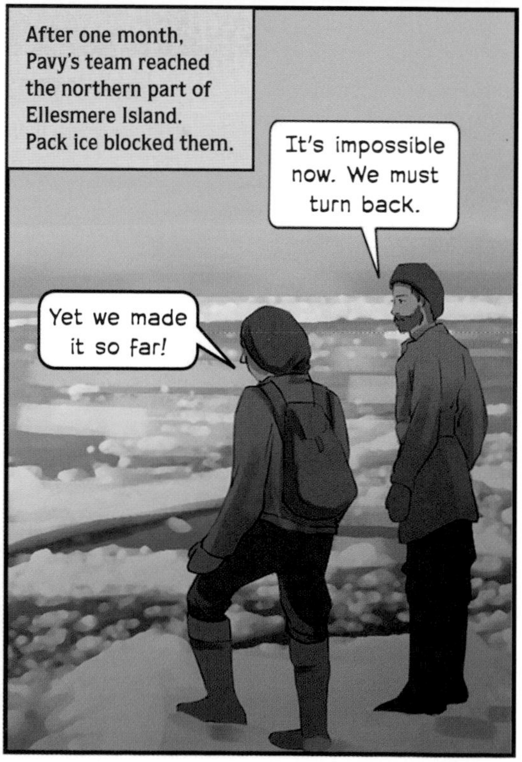
After one month, Pavy's team reached the northern part of Ellesmere Island. Pack ice blocked them.
It's impossible now. We must turn back.
Yet we made it so far!

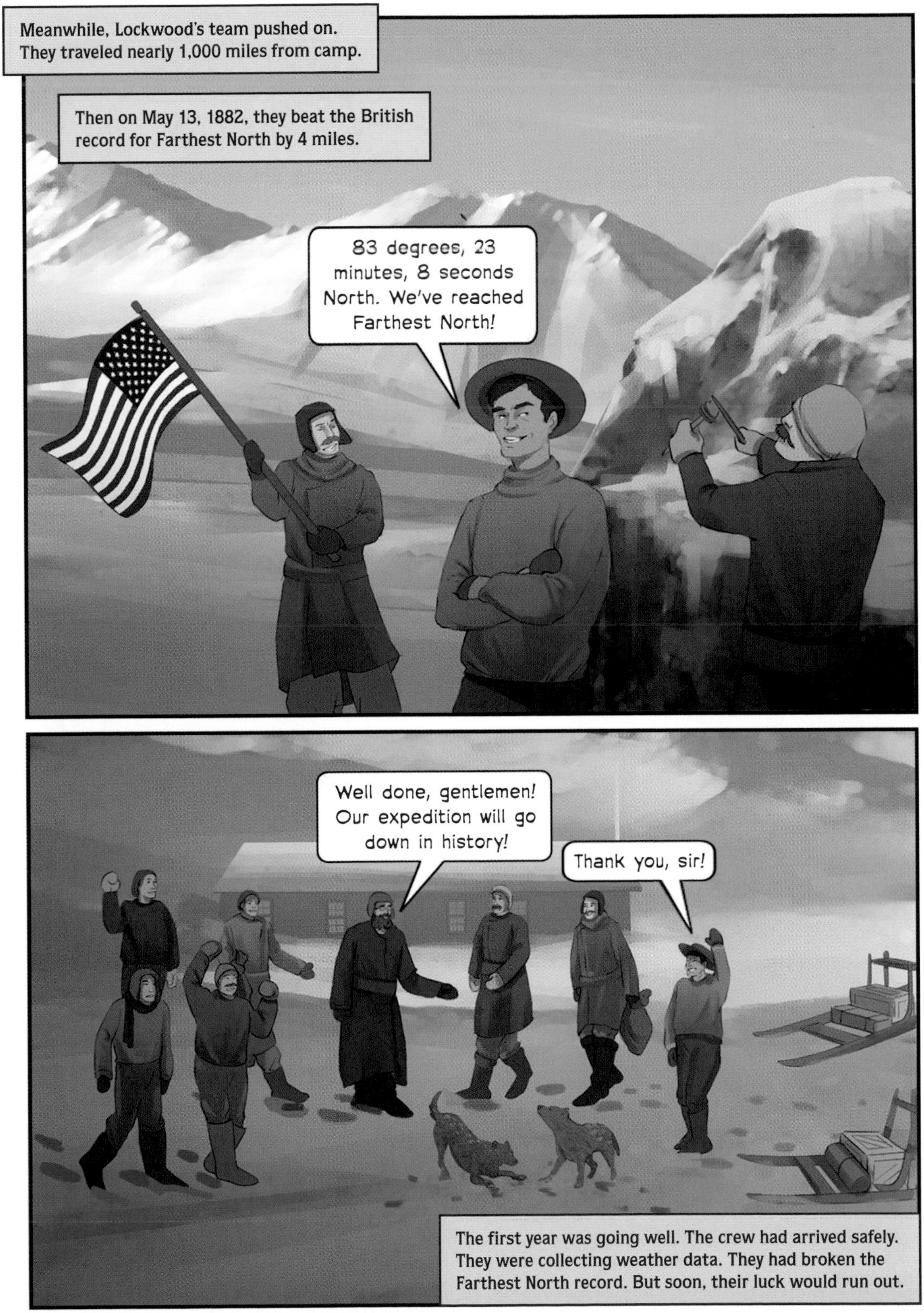
Meanwhile, Lockwood's team pushed on. They traveled nearly 1,000 miles from camp.
Then on May 13, 1882, they beat the British record for Farthest North by 4 miles.
83 degrees, 23 minutes, 8 seconds North. We've reached Farthest North!
Well done, gentlemen! Our expedition will go down in history!
Thank you, sir!
The first year was going well. The crew had arrived safely. They were collecting weather data. They had broken the Farthest North record. But soon, their luck would run out.

As summer drew closer, the crew watched for the promised supply ship. June turned into July. When August arrived, they realized a ship was not coming.

I have faith in our government. A ship will come next summer.

I fear there will be no ship then either.

I fear this too.

The *Neptune* had tried to reach the expedition team. The ship had left St. John's on July 8, 1882.

But ice filled the waters. This forced the ship to stop at Littleton Island and Cape Sabine, 250 miles away from Fort Conger. The crew unloaded a small food supply.

Just leave a few crates. They have plenty of animals to hunt!

NEPTUNE

Fall turned into winter. The men at Fort Conger faced a grim reality.

We'll have to make do with what we have.

They hunted for extra food. But it was difficult. Walking through snowstorms was tiring. Wind and blowing snow made it hard to spot animals.

This bear will not last us very long.

I cannot bring myself to regret coming. I shall at least have made my mark in the world.

I miss you so much . . .

The crew could not send letters. Still, Greely wrote to his wife through the winter.

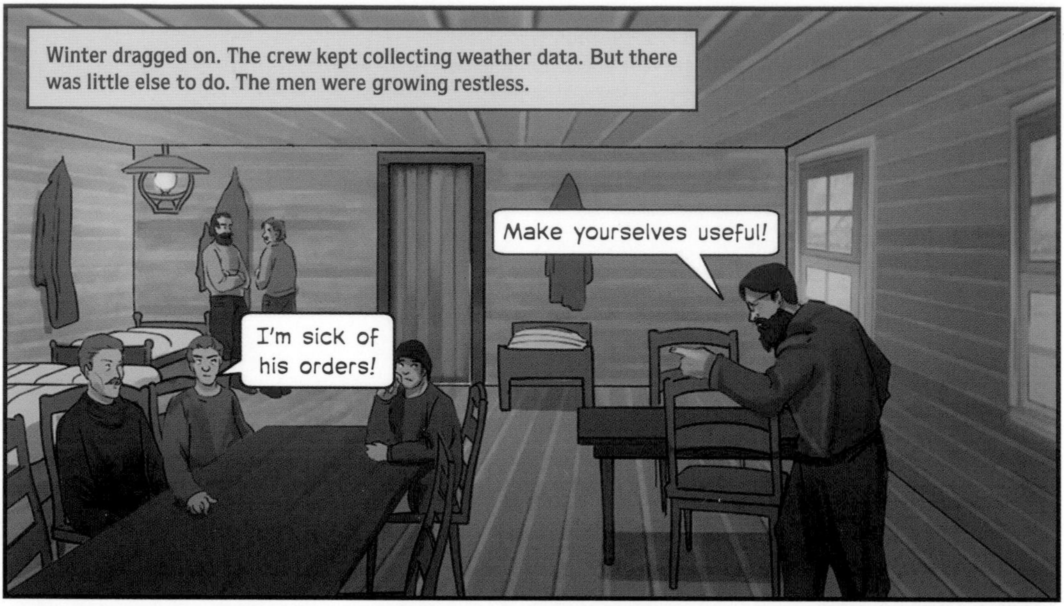
Winter dragged on. The crew kept collecting weather data. But there was little else to do. The men were growing restless.
Make yourselves useful!
I'm sick of his orders!

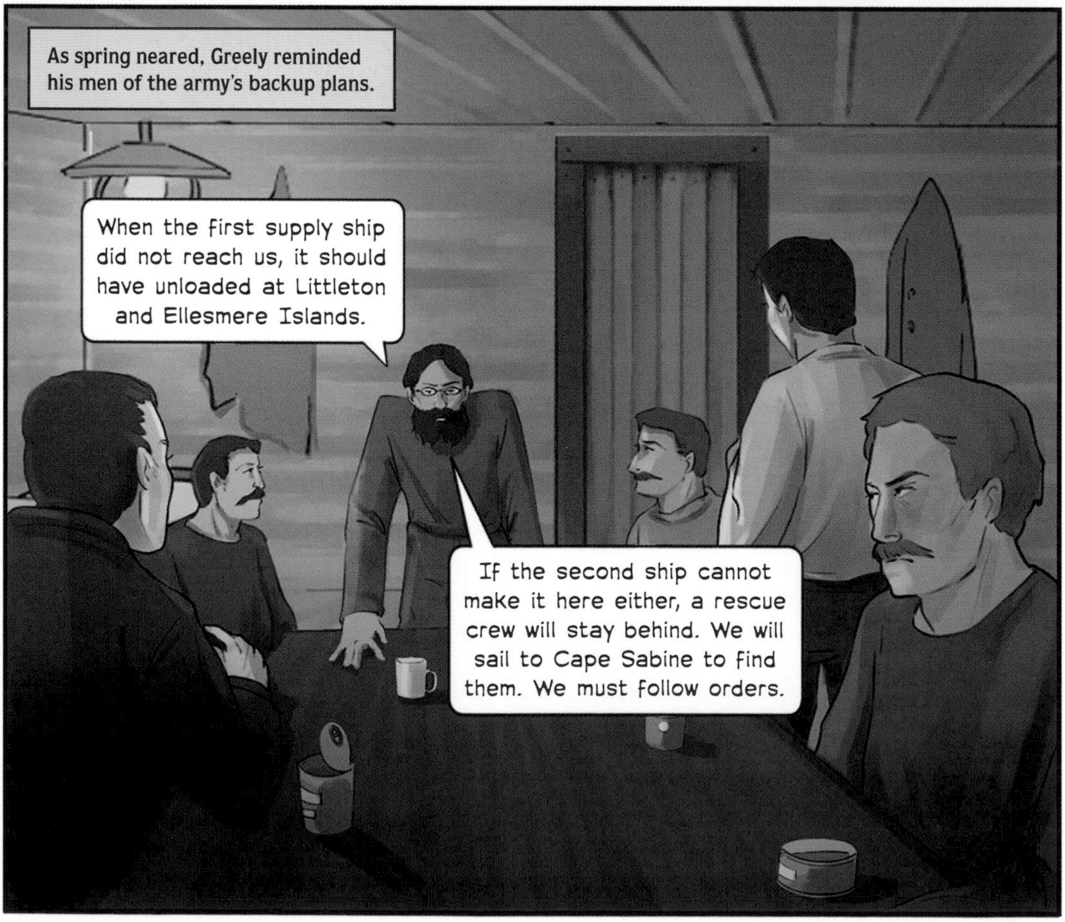
As spring neared, Greely reminded his men of the army's backup plans.
When the first supply ship did not reach us, it should have unloaded at Littleton and Ellesmere Islands.
If the second ship cannot make it here either, a rescue crew will stay behind. We will sail to Cape Sabine to find them. We must follow orders.

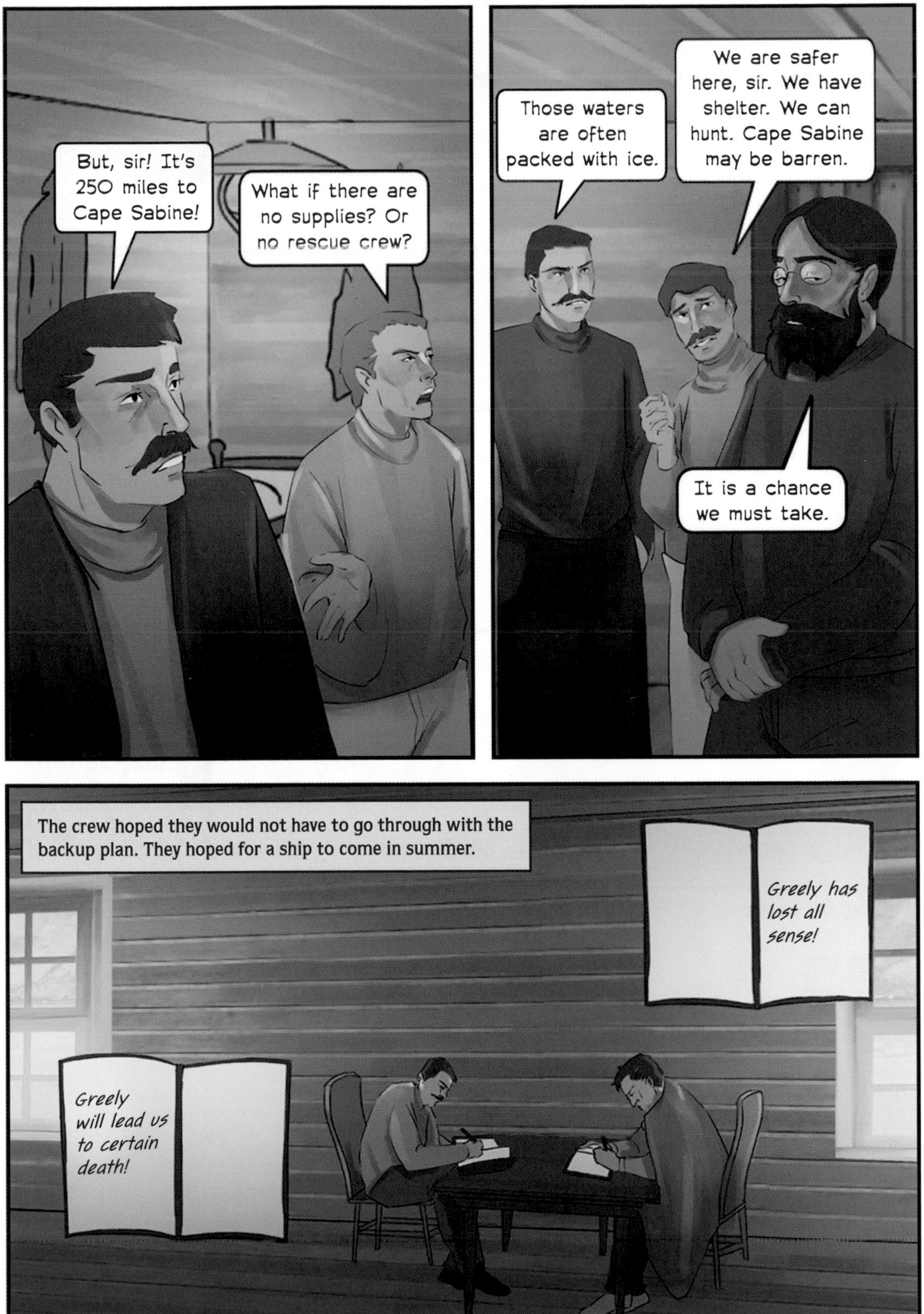

But, sir! It's 250 miles to Cape Sabine!
What if there are no supplies? Or no rescue crew?
Those waters are often packed with ice.
We are safer here, sir. We have shelter. We can hunt. Cape Sabine may be barren.
It is a chance we must take.
The crew hoped they would not have to go through with the backup plan. They hoped for a ship to come in summer.
Greely has lost all sense!
Greely will lead us to certain death!

On June 28, 1883, the *Proteus* left for Fort Conger. It was supposed to bring the expedition team home.

Sail around it!

Sir, there is too much ice!

But the ship sank with most supplies on board.

Abandon ship!

Tell them that my crew is saved . . . all well!

We are returning home.

The *Proteus* crew drifted in small boats for 40 days. They were rescued. But afterward, no one wanted to wait for Greely and his men.

Despite their low food supplies, the men at Fort Conger had survived the winter.

Summer arrived. The ship didn't. So, Greely decided to act. He ordered the crew to pack for Cape Sabine.

On August 9, 1883, the team left Fort Conger. They took some food, supplies, and their weather records.

Many of the men were angry. They still felt it was a mistake to leave Fort Conger.

Do as I say, or you shall be shot!

Greely has lost his mind!

Greely also began to doubt his choice to leave. He rested in the steamboat for hours. Sergeant Rice was left to guide the crew.

Slowly, men! Watch the ice!

What have I done?

One night, as Greely slept, three men spoke with Brainard.

Greely has no plan!

We must turn back!

The doctor says he can declare Greely insane. Another officer can take command.

We can return to Fort Conger!

To turn back now is out of the question. We must advance, although I am fearful it will result in disaster.

Brainard refused to go against Greely. The idea was forgotten.

Two weeks later, the crew's steamboat became stuck in ice. But they needed to keep moving. They pulled their whaleboats and supplies onto an ice floe.

The men faced bad weather. They floated on the ice through fierce storms.

After 51 days, they managed to reach Eskimo Point below Cape Sabine. Everyone had survived the journey.

There was no rescue party in sight on Cape Sabine. Instead, Greely and his men found a note from the failed supply mission.

The *Proteus* sank. They have left us three crates of food.

That will last us only a few weeks!

Greely still hoped rescuers would come. In any case, the men could not make the trip back to Fort Conger. So, the crew settled in. They built a hut named Camp Clay.

Greely regained focus. He prepared his men to face a third Arctic winter. Many were now glad for his leadership.

There are few animals to hunt here. We must ration food.

Yes, sir.

Yes, sir.

Yes, sir.

In November, Rice led a small search party to look for food left by other expeditions. They walked for 30 miles over five days. The group found boxes of dried meat. As they hurried back, one man got severe frostbite.

Leave the food. We must carry Ellison instead!

Soon, the exhausted group could not go any farther. Rice went on alone. He walked for 12 hours till he reached camp and got help.

Everyone in the search party was brought back.

Give Ellison extra food. He needs it more than us.

The harsh weather made it impossible to go out for the meat again. There were almost no animals to hunt or plants to eat. The men began to starve.

On January 18, 1884, the expedition had its first death. One man died of scurvy.

Farewell, Cross.

Rice was determined to help the team survive. He walked long distances looking for a rescue party. He began catching shrimp. It wasn't much, but any food was welcomed.

Still, the men struggled. Many had frostbite. Their food supplies were extremely low. In March, one man was caught taking food. Greely warned that anyone found stealing again would be shot. At the start of April, two men died of starvation.

On April 7, Rice and Frederick left Camp Clay. They were searching for the boxes of meat they had left behind months earlier. A storm forced them to take shelter.

When the storm ended, they set out again. Suddenly, Rice collapsed.

Rice! What's going on?

Rest in peace, my friend.

Rice is gone.

After burying Rice, Frederick returned to camp. He came back empty-handed. He had not been able to carry the boxes of food by himself.

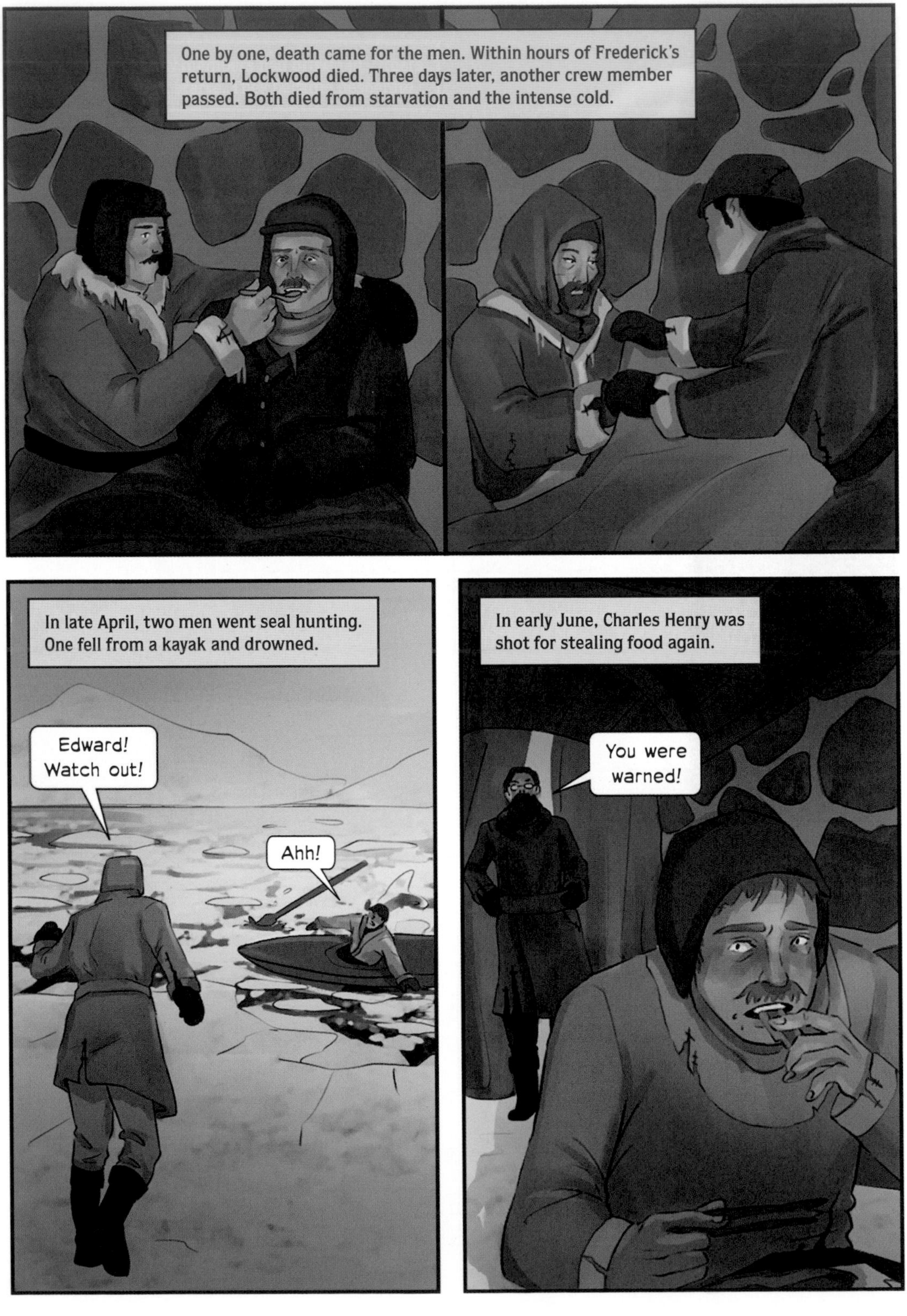
One by one, death came for the men. Within hours of Frederick's return, Lockwood died. Three days later, another crew member passed. Both died from starvation and the intense cold.
In late April, two men went seal hunting. One fell from a kayak and drowned.
Edward! Watch out!
Ahh!
In early June, Charles Henry was shot for stealing food again.
You were warned!

By mid-June, 18 men had died. The crew had almost no food. They were eating candle wax, shoe leather, and moldy dog biscuits.

Greely's attitude toward his men softened. He helped however he could.

To die is easy . . . it is only hard to strive, to endure, to live.

While Greely and his men suffered, Henrietta Greely was trying to help them. After the *Proteus* sank, she wrote to the government. She asked them to send another rescue ship. Her letters were ignored.

Mr. Greely expressed to me complete faith in the government's care for its own expedition.

Many officials believed the expedition team was fine.

Hunting and rationing should keep the men comfortable through the winter.

We can send a ship next spring.

They have abandoned those poor men!

Trapped in Arctic, Horrible Sufferings

Henrietta went to the press. Embarrassed by the newspaper stories, the government agreed to act. In April, three rescue ships set sail.

On June 22, 1884, rescuers reached Cape Sabine. They had expected to find 25 healthy men.

Instead, they found seven sickly survivors. Greely and his crew had been stuck there for nine months.

Greely, is this you?

The rescuers gathered the team's scientific records. They exhumed the bodies of the dead. The expedition members, both dead and alive, were finally going home.

On August 1, the rescue ship arrived at Portsmouth Harbor, New Hampshire. Ellison had died during the trip. The six remaining survivors were greeted as heroes.

They had carried out their scientific work, reached Farthest North, and survived despite the odds.

I have missed you so.

Welcome home!

The army, however, was not so happy. They believed the expedition had hurt the army's reputation. They questioned Greely's choices.

I wished to save my men, sir.

You left the safety of Fort Conger! And you ordered a man shot! Why?

Rumors also spread. Doctors found cuts on some dead crew members' bodies. Newspapers said this proved the men had eaten the dead to survive. Greely and the others denied all rumors of cannibalism.

What a terrible thing to do!

Greely stayed determined to honor his crew. He spent the next several years publishing the team's research.

The world would learn about the sacrifices and achievements of the Greely expedition.

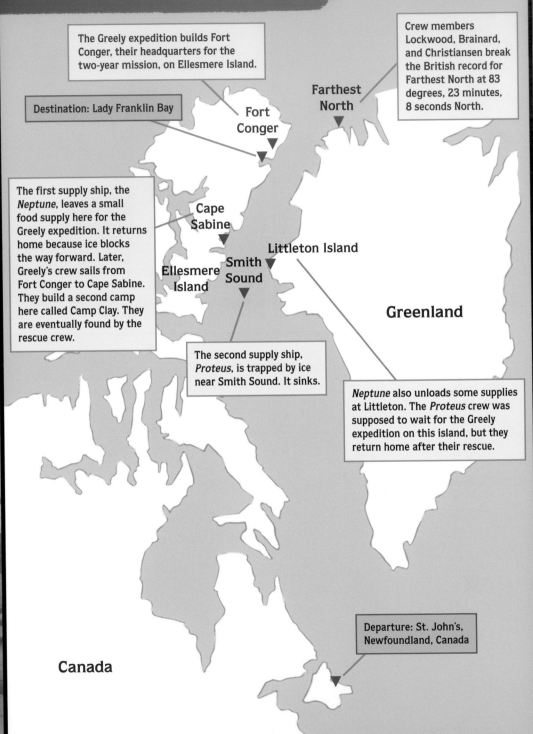

The Greely expedition builds Fort Conger, their headquarters for the two-year mission, on Ellesmere Island.

Crew members Lockwood, Brainard, and Christiansen break the British record for Farthest North at 83 degrees, 23 minutes, 8 seconds North.

Destination: Lady Franklin Bay

Farthest North ▼

Fort Conger ▼

The first supply ship, the *Neptune*, leaves a small food supply here for the Greely expedition. It returns home because ice blocks the way forward. Later, Greely's crew sails from Fort Conger to Cape Sabine. They build a second camp here called Camp Clay. They are eventually found by the rescue crew.

Cape Sabine ▼

Littleton Island

Smith Sound ▼

Ellesmere Island

Greenland

The second supply ship, *Proteus*, is trapped by ice near Smith Sound. It sinks.

Neptune also unloads some supplies at Littleton. The *Proteus* crew was supposed to wait for the Greely expedition on this island, but they return home after their rescue.

Departure: St. John's, Newfoundland, Canada

Canada

MORE ABOUT THE EXPEDITION

The polar expedition survivors faced difficult times after their rescue. Upset by the cannibalism rumors and Greely's decisions, the army ignored the men's scientific research. They did not pay the men's salaries for years. Slowly, the army began to recognize the achievements of the survivors. Each man was given a promotion. Greely refused one.

Little by little, the survivors returned to normal life. Maurice Connell, Julius Frederick, and Henry Biederbick all went on to work for the U.S. Weather Bureau. David Brainard stayed in the military. Eventually, he wrote two books about the journey to Lady Franklin Bay. Francis Long went on another polar expedition.

Adolphus Greely stayed in the army until he retired. Over time, Greely gained praise for his leadership in the Arctic. He received the Congressional Medal of Honor in 1935. It was just months before his death.

The expedition's research had been part of a larger effort called the First International Polar Year. The work of Greely and his men plays an important role in modern-day research. Scientists of today can look back at the weather data from nearly a century ago. They can compare it to recent data. The research of the Greely expedition is helping scientists understand how Earth's climate is changing.

GLOSSARY

barren (BER-ren)—growing little to no plants

cannibalism (KAN-uh-buh-liz-uhm)—the act of a person eating the flesh of another person

exhume (ig-ZOOM)—to take a dead body out of the place it was buried

expedition (ek-spuh-DIH-shuhn)—a journey with a goal, such as exploring or searching for something

frostbite (FRAWST-bahyt)—the freezing of skin on some part of the body due to cold temperatures

funding (FUN-ding)—money that is given to a group or person and is to be used for a specific purpose

Inuit (IN-yoo-it)—the native people of Alaska and other northern and Arctic regions

latitude (LAT-ih-tood)—a distance north or south from the equator, measured in degrees

ration (RASH-uhn)—to give out something in small amounts in order to keep it from running out

scurvy (SKUR-vee)—a deadly disease caused by lack of vitamin C; scurvy causes swollen limbs, bleeding gums, and weakness

telegraph (TEL-uh-graf)—an electric device or system for sending messages by a code over wires

READ MORE

Enz, Tammy. *Science on Shackleton's Expedition.* North Mankato, MN: Capstone, 2022.

Huang, Nellie. *Explorers: Amazing Tales of the World's Greatest Adventurers.* New York: DK Publishing, 2019.

Rea, Amy C. *Race to the Poles.* Mankato, MN: The Child's World, 2020.

INTERNET SITES

DK FindOut!: Polar Explorers
dkfindout.com/us/history/explorers/polar-explorers/

National Geographic Kids: 10 Facts About the Arctic!
natgeokids.com/uk/discover/geography/general-geography/ten-facts-about-the-arctic/

Science and Survival at Fort Conger
fortconger.org/index

AUTHOR BIO

Golriz Golkar is the author of more than 60 nonfiction and fiction books for children. Inspired by her work as an elementary school teacher, she loves to write the kinds of books that students are excited to read. Golriz holds a B.A. in American literature and culture from UCLA and an Ed.M. in language and literacy from the Harvard Graduate School of Education. Golriz lives in France with her husband and young daughter.

ILLUSTRATOR BIO

Ana Carolina Tega is a Brazilian digital artist. She is an undergraduate student from the University of Hertfordshire and is currently studying 3D games art and design. She also works in the entertainment industry for short film production. Her body of work includes developing 3D assets for games, creating concept art for films, and illustrating for the publishing market. Today, she is part of the Storm Creative Studio artist team.